The Fred Book

The Fred Book

Fred Imus

with Mike Lupica

Doubleday

New York London Toronto Sydney Auckland

PUBLISHED BY DOUBLEDAY
a division of Bantam Doubleday Dell Publishing Group, Inc.
1540 Broadway, New York, New York 10036

DOUBLEDAY and the portrayal of an anchor with a dolphin are
trademarks of Doubleday, a division of Bantam Doubleday Dell
Publishing Group, Inc.

Library of Congress Cataloging-in-Publication Data

Imus, Fred.
The Fred book / Fred Imus with Mike Lupica. — 1st ed.
p.   cm.
1. American wit and humor. I. Lupica, Mike.
II. Title.
PN6162.I49   1998
818'.5407—DC21   98-15393
CIP

ISBN 0-385-47652-3
Printed in the United States of America
June 1998
First Edition

Book design by Judith Stagnitto Abbate

1 3 5 7 9 10 8 6 4 2

Contents

for Four-Legged Fred

Introduction

Clearly Mike Lupica and my brother, Fred Imus, asked me to write an introduction for their book hoping I'd come up with something funny—because as you are about to discover, *they* didn't.

Jesus, what a mess.

You would think that between two people— my brother, who's not exactly a moron, and Lupica, who *is*, after all, a professional writer— something amusing would have even *accidentally* found its way onto a page in this piece of shit. It did not.

How then did this become a book? "Book" in the loosest sense of that word, may I add?

It pretty much happened this way:

Greedy New York book publisher offers Fred cash advance to write book.

Fred takes cash.

Writes nothing.

Book publisher assigns editor to call Fred and ask about book.

Fred ignores editor.

Editor calls me.

I think call is about book *I* owe them.

I ignore call.

Enter Lupica.

Make that, Enter a *greedy* Lupica. He offers to interview Fred and write book *for* Fred. He does.

Problem.

Lupica writes down what Fred actually says. It is beyond idiotic.

Fred tries to fix it.

Lupica tries to fix it.

I try to fix it.

We all fail.

Now, it's your fucking problem.

- - - - - -

Preface

▬ ▬ ▬ ▬ ▬ ▬ ▬ ▬ ▬

Now that the Auto
Body Express has turned into a million-dollar operation—or for the purposes of my tax returns,
what you would call your struggling small business—people ask me all the time if I have any
secrets. The truth is I have two, and they're both
equally important if you want to parlay a bunch
of T-shirts into a big-time mail order operation
that includes everything from denim work shirts
to salsa and cologne. I'll try not to get too techni-
cal with this, but here they are:

1. Have a brother on the radio.
2. Don't be afraid to pick up the phone.

Everything that's happened in the last few years
started with the phone ringing. Don told people to

▬ ▬ ▬ ▬ ▬

call me in El Paso and order up one of these T-shirts we'd made so I could buy some of the automobile parts I desperately needed to keep fixin' cars. At that time, I was restoring '57 Chevys and selling automotive paint to body shops, one exit up from a trailer park. The whole operation was Bob and me. I used to buy my tools from Bob, and decided that if I ever had a business of my own, I'd hire him. Neither one of us was making any money, but Bob was a positive-type person, I liked him, and I liked restoring cars once I taught myself how. I'd done a little bit of everything else. I'd worked on the Southern Pacific Railroad for ten years, had been a disc jockey and had even written some country songs. One of them, "I Don't Want to Have to Marry You," went to Number One in the seventies and made me more money—about a hundred thousand dollars—than I'd ever made before or ever expected to make again. It is probably worth pointing out right here that all of the money I made from "I Don't Want to Have to Marry You" was gone, like most of my hair, by 1991.

Anyway, we needed parts and Don and I came up with the idea for selling a few T-shirts on the radio. He gave the phone number and told people what the shirts looked like and what they'd cost. His show wasn't nationally syndicated the way it is now, but it still had a huge audience in

— — — — — —

New York, New Jersey, and Connecticut. He talked about the shirts for a while, and the next day as I was opening up shop, both phones were ringing.

Bob and I didn't do anything but answer the phones that day. As we were ready to close, Bob said, "You know, I think this deal might last."

I told him he was full of shit, being the straightforward person that I am.

"Today and tomorrow," I said. "Then it'll be over."

"You're wrong," he said.

"We'll see."

We sold out the original order of shirts by the second day and ordered more. By the end of the first week, we had to hire more people just to answer the phones and take orders. At first, people would call and I'd ask for their address and then I'd send them the shirts, they could send the money later. By about noon, I began to figure out that maybe that wasn't the brightest way to build your business empire. And by late afternoon, I was telling folks to send a check, they'd get the shirts when I got the money. I think that was Tuesday. By Friday, the checks started to roll in. I'd go over to the post office and get one of those big baskets they give you over there and basically just fill them up with money. At night, I'd sit in the apart-

------

ment and separate the checks by state. Don called me up one of the first nights and asked me what I was doing.

"Counting Connecticut money," I said.

He asked me what I meant.

"Seeing if it's more than the Jersey money, or the New York money," I said.

"How much is there?" he asked.

"About three post office baskets' worth today," I said.

We had started out with orders of two hundred shirts. The next one was for two thousand. By the end of the first month, we were ordering five thousand shirts at a time. Ten thousand after that. We sold the first batch for seventeen dollars apiece, until one day when I was taking orders and a caller said, "You like to fix up those 1957 Chevys, right?"

I told him I did, not that I was doing much repairing lately.

"Why don't you sell those shirts of yours for nineteen fifty-seven."

We started to charge $19.57 the very next day, and have used variations of that price on everything we've sold since. Another free business tip: Don't just pick up the phone. Listen. It works.

And trust me on something else: Most of what follows in this book is as true as I can make it, whether it's about running a business, dealing with ex-wives, *Monday Night Football*, or my

- - - - - -

brother Don. I guess you could say I've always figured things out along the way, telling the truth as
often as I could, bullshitting when I had to, trying
to make some sense of life, politics, country music,
big-time radio, sex, money, women, children, polit-
ical correctness, whether or not to put those little
paper tops on the salsa bottles, and just about every other amusing aspect of what you would call
your American way.

As an old football player named Alex Haw-
kins used to say: This is my story. And I'm stick-
ing to it.

Part ✦ One

The
Auto Body
Express

Occasionally, Don and I talk about taking the Auto Body Express public. Between the Andrews Brothers (our financial advisors) and my brother's crooked Wall Street friends, we figure we'd make a killing.

Except I look at going public as simply providing an opportunity for a bunch of pushy assholes to come in and tell me how to run my business.

And as I said to Don, I already have one asshole telling me what to do. He was not amused.

- - - - - -

I still take orders my own self, as Dan Jenkins says.

I just don't take them quite as fast—or as well—as some of the other people I've got working for me. Every time I ask somebody to spell the name of a difficult-sounding city, there's always this pause on the other end of the line. Finally, they'll ask, "This is Fred, isn't it?"

Like they're talking to Fred Gump.

I like the Pope about as much as anybody who's not Catholic. In fact, probably more than some Catholics, now that I think about it.

Take priests and the celibacy deal, for example. We're not all that far apart.

I *have* wondered why the Catholics didn't get in on the kosher food scam though. Especially for Lent. That's a huge market.

Catholics—they really do need more Jews calling the shots on the business side.

- - - - - -

Jesus, have I had my share of hideous help at the Auto Body Express. I've hired people who were stupid. And some who were flat-out crooks. And some who were both. And when you get a combination like that going—dumb and dishonest—if you don't pay attention, they can make the whole operation come crashing down around your ears.

Hey, if you don't believe me, just ask the President. Of course, in his case, it's down around his ankles.

I still miss working on those '57 Chevys. Actually, they didn't have to be '57 Chevys, they could have been any of those old cars I used to fix up at the Fred Imus Car Gallery. There was something about restoring those cars that I just loved. Even back in high school I lusted after a particular '56 Ford pickup that needed an overhaul. I loved everything about cars. It wasn't just restoring them, I loved taking them apart all the way down to the frame and basically starting over. When I first tried it, I didn't know much more than how to give a car a tune-up, but I asked a lot of questions and learned as I went.

Sort of like I did with the T-shirts. It used to take me about a year to restore a car. About the same length of time it takes to receive something you've ordered from the Auto Body Express.

Some things never change.

- - - - - -

I'm not what you would call a real clothes horse. Put it another way, don't wait around for me to start modeling clothes for the Auto Body Express the way Ralph Lauren does with his tweed suits and Polo ponies. My favorite article of clothing is whatever boots are next to the bed and whichever jeans are next to them. The rest of it I don't pay very much attention to. I actually have shirts so old they go back to when Phyllis and I were still married. I always sort of suspected those shirts were going to outlast Phyllis.

And it's unlikely I'm going to make anybody's best-dressed list either, even though I'm in the clothing business. I don't own a suit. I don't own a sports jacket. I don't own a single tie, though we sell some beauties designed by Joseph Abboud (and that number again is 800-272-1957). I have

- - - - - - -

8

exactly three pairs of jeans at any given time and shirts that go back to the Dark Ages when I was married to Phyllis, like I said. That's it, other than T-shirts, boots, and baseball caps.

If clothes make the man, I'm screwed.

I just never thought Princess Diana would turn out to be another Elvis. But that's exactly what happened, even though you never could have seen it coming while she was alive, the way you did with Elvis. I suppose I followed her life about as well as anyone who doesn't read *People* magazine on a regular basis could. But it wasn't until she died in that car wreck that I realized the whole world was about half in love with her.

That burial site deal they've come up with for her? I just can tell it's going to be the English version of Graceland. I only hope they can manage to do it without selling a bunch of tacky shit like they do with Elvis.

Of course, if they'd like to put a turquoise buffalo on the Diana T-shirts, that's another matter altogether.

- - - - - -

I'm hoping that someday I can turn the Auto Body Express over to my kids, make it a real family business. My son Donny has been working for me for a couple of years now, and shows some real promise.

Of course, he'll have to avoid the pull of heredity and try not to screw around with the female help. Right now he's doing about as well as the President.

I've never sent money to a single television evangelist. Now, I don't have anything against them. They're just like other people, in my opinion, which means some of them are good and some of them are full of shit. And I know there are lots of people who think they're good, because they're the ones sending Jimmy Swaggart millions of dollars.

My feeling is, if you feel like reaching for the phone, why not call me instead.

- - - - - - -

Aside from the Auto Body Express, my other full-time job is telling my brother he should never retire. I usually make the observation when I see what happens to our orders when he takes some time off. I'll say to him, "You have the best radio show that has ever been on the air, why would you want to give it all up?" Or, "What would you do with yourself if you ever retired?"

One thing he would do is move out here and bitch at me full-time.

A while back, a New York newspaper guy wrote how much he liked Don's show and pointed out that I was his best guest. And so I'm thinking, Tim Russert, Tom Brokaw, Doris Kearns Goodwin, and all the rest of them can kiss my ass . . . that's what I'm thinking.

———————

Every time I think of the IRS, especially now that I'm making a little money at the Auto Body Express, there's one image I can't get out of my mind.

Unfortunately, the image is the one of the cops pulling poor old Rodney King out of the car.

Every once in a while, when Don does take a vacation and the phones don't ring as regularly as I like, I actually do start looking in the want ads, just the way I used to before the Auto Body Express got rolling. And I don't have any more success finding something I'm qualified to do than I ever did. Let me put it another way: I'm more scared of my brother retiring than I would be with a nuclear face-off between us and Saddam Hussein. You know why? The result is exactly the same for me.

I'm dead.

I'm never retiring. And the reason I have for myself is the same as I have for my brother. I don't know what I'd do with myself. In other words, I really don't have any long-range retirement plans. But then, I've never had any long-range plans of any kind.

I just kind of go football season to football season, and hope for the best.

The way I look at things, the whole country seems to be for sale. From the White House down. If somebody had told you twenty years ago that CBS would be sold, you would have laughed. Or the Dodgers. I never thought NBC radio would ever be for sale. But everything is. You pick up the paper one day and find out that Hilton is going after ITT/Sheraton and all its holdings—including Madison Square Garden and the New York Knicks and the New York Rangers—and you feel as if you read a story exactly like it the day before, about some other mogul and some other company. But you know what's not for sale?

The Auto Body Express.

And I'll tell you why: I don't ever want to have to get another job.

— — — — — — —

Part ★ Two

I-Man

Don and I grew up on a ranch in northern Arizona, near Kingman. My father also had a feedlot he owned in California. Until the time Don and I were in high school, it was just the two of us on the farm. We didn't have any real friends, other than the various farm animals. Just because my brother was real good with the horses and cows, I don't think there should be nearly as much malicious gossip floating around out there about him and livestock. He sure did have a good rapport with them, though.

He'll probably deny it, but I think he still sends some of them cards on their birthdays.

- - - - - -

The news that scientists had figured out a way to clone sheep touched off all these legal, moral, and ethical arguments that frankly confused the shit out of me. When I saw the pictures in the paper, I was just glad they cloned a pretty one. You grow up where my brother and I did, and you'd never be able to understand why anyone would feel the need to clone sheep.

With all the cute ones we had on the ranch, it's a miracle either one of us ever left home.

– – – – – –

You know one person I'd actually like to see cloned?

O.J.

Then he'd have to spend the rest of his life looking over his shoulder, wondering when his double was going to jump out of the bushes in a ski mask and Bruno Magli shoes and take *his* ass out.

You know what safe sex is on a farm, by the way?

Painting a big red "X" on the animals that kick.

My brother is very particular about having stuff be in its place and having stuff be put away. That's why I look forward to his visits to Santa Fe. It's another opportunity for me to drive him insane. Remember that old movie *Gaslight*, where the husband slowly tries to convince his wife that she's crazy? I do it to Don by leaving open containers of food on the kitchen counter. It doesn't matter that my brother has the biggest and best show in the history of radio, I can bring him to his knees with just one jar of Hellmann's mayonnaise.

Left open on the counter, that is.

- - - - - -

My brother is a
world-class photographer. He's very particular—big surprise there—and he wants things to be exactly right. The weather's got to be right. The lighting has to be just right. If there's a shot to be found in a particular place, Don will find it. Why am I telling you this?

Don wants me to.

I don't drink anymore. Don used to drink so much that when he quit, I went right along with him. You've heard the expression that somebody drank enough for two people? And the one Hillary Clinton keeps talking about, it takes a village?

Well, my brother drank enough for two people and we both drank enough for a village.

My brother is one of those people with hair who are always telling people like me without hair how great we look. How being bald shouldn't bother us. How women don't care whether men have hair or not. My brother is also one of those people who act as if bald people don't have mirrors. I can look in the mirror anytime I want to and see that I look like shit.

People who tell you being bald doesn't matter are like the guys who tell you women don't care how long your penis is. Sure they don't. In my experience, those are generally the guys whose wives or girlfriends are off somewhere seeing if they can make Wilt's list, or Bill Clinton's. Though I can vouch for the fact that there are some women who don't care if a guy is bald—the older ones. I think they care less about things like hair

- - - - - -

once they get past thirty. Once a woman gets up there, she really doesn't give a damn whether you've any hair on your head.

They get past forty, they don't even care whether you've got a head.

I don't have any problem with somebody spending the money to try one of those hair replacement deals if being bald matters that much to them. Don thinks it's stupid and is always making fun of guys with hair plugs or the Marv Alberts of the world. Hell, if it makes you feel better about yourself and you can afford it, go for it. I'm just not all that sure that the last thirty years would have gone all that differently for me if I'd had a full head of hair.

Other than all the money I would have saved on baseball caps.

- - - - - - -

I guess the two most successful relationships I've ever had in my life are with Four-Legged Fred and my two-legged brother. There are a lot of similarities between them. The biggest one is that neither one wears you out with a lot of idle chatter. There is one pretty significant difference, though: when my brother gets mad at me he doesn't piss on the corner of the bed.

At least not anymore.

Part Three

Irreconcilable

Differences

Marriage to me is un-natural. Men and women aren't meant to live with each other. I believe we should be more like the animal kingdom. Lions, for example. The male lion really only comes around when he wants to get laid. Then he just wanders around for the rest of the year.

What, you have a problem with that?

- - - - - -

There are some guys who work here at the Auto Body Express who are very sexist. Some would even go so far as to say that women should never have been allowed to vote. I mean, how can anybody be that reactionary as we move on up to the end of what you call your twentieth century? Hasn't anybody learned a single goddamn thing over the last hundred years? Is there any question whether women should be allowed to vote? Shit. They should absolutely be allowed to vote.

Whether the votes should count is another matter entirely.

- - - - - - -

I was able to figure out that my marriage to Phyllis was failing by the growing frequency of times I would come home to find my belongings on the front lawn. In the early days of our marriage, it was about once every three months. It sort of escalated from there to about once a month. Then once a week. I was married for exactly ten years and three days. Which means my clothes were flung outside a total of about two hundred and fifty-six times. I don't know who keeps records on this sort of thing, but if you're talking about consistency and a high-level of performance of pissing your spouse off, I'm Michael Jordan.

In other words, my marriage to Phyllis looked like one long garage sale.

- - - - - -

I get a big kick when I hear or read about prenuptial agreements. I know that Donald Trump, in his book, is supposed to go on and on about how having a good prenup is some sort of key to being a success in life, after you've tried to fuck it up by marring an Ivana or a Marla. You want to know what my prenup was with Phyllis?

She got everything.

Well, that's not exactly correct. When she finally kicked me out, I got everything I could fit into my '65 Chevy Impala.

Actually, when I think back on that happy day, the Impala wasn't even that full.

As a husband, I rate myself a 4 on a scale of 10.

I would have graded out a lot higher if I'd shown up for work just a little more often than I did.

There is nothing harder in this world, nothing even close, than being a parent. I have four children, and the more kids Phyllis and I had, the more I became convinced of that. Even as I was trying to come up with what I consider some very handy tips for parents, I couldn't help but reflect on how even the most simple things, like going to a restaurant, are a trial. So here's my advice, such as it is: Never take your children to a restaurant.

Ever.

If you absolutely have to, don't go until they are at least eight years old. Even then, prepare to spend the whole night crawling around under tables and picking up shit they've spilled. Try not to take them out again until they're around eighteen. (If you're lucky, they won't want to have anything to do with you by then.)

I'm not sure this is the way a child psychologist would see things, but this advice has always worked for me.

- - - - - - -

Every once in a while, I'll turn on the television and hear some conversation on the evening news about whether or not there's this deal called the "gay gene." As though whether you're going to like boys or girls is decided for you, and that heredity and environment and the rest of that shit has nothing to do with it. I think there might be something to that, where you're just born with an aptitude for something. Like being able to completely screw up a marriage, for example. Until I started thinking about this gene business, I just assumed you stumbled into something like that.

Now I realize it was just a gift.

———————

I can admit now that I was never very good with diapers. Putting them on or taking them off. But especially taking them off. If my wife left me with the kids for a few days, she'd come home and generally find them walking around with their diapers dragging on the floor as if they were loaded down with bricks. The first time it happened, she started yelling and asking me just what I thought I was doing.

I told her that when I saw "10–12 pounds" on the diaper box, I thought that meant how much they could hold.

- - - - - -

What I've learned as I've gotten older is that having and raising kids is a lot easier when you're able to pay the bills. Lights and water, for example. You know, the old fundamentals. A hundred different doctors can write a hundred different books about child rearing, but if the lights and water are off and you can't even *see* your kids, or wash them . . . you sure as hell can't teach 'em shit.

——————

You know what there really should be for anybody who wants to be a parent?

A test.

You should have to pass a test to become a parent the same way you do before you get a driver's license.

If you have a problem with this, I just have two words to say: Michael Jackson.

- - - - - -

In the old days, the father used to pace and smoke and the mother would go into the delivery room and have the damn baby. I forget which one of our kids it was, but I told Phyllis in the doctor's office that if they really wanted me to come into the delivery room, I would. But I was still going to smoke.

Actually, I kind of did like going into the delivery room. I mean, you know there's something in there. But you can never be sure exactly what.

———————

Despite the fact that I'm never getting married again, I'm a firm believer that monogamy does work. As far as I'm concerned, if you still want to screw around, there's no reason to get married in the first place.

Unless, of course, you want to grow up to be the leader of the free world, with the White House intern staff looking like a bigger athletic challenge than the Olympics.

- - - - - -

It wasn't until after Phyllis and I got divorced that I found out that a woman's premenstrual syndrome didn't last for thirty-day cycles.

Phyllis also used to get a kick out of me when I'd bitch at one of our boys about not working hard enough or applying himself to some kind of job. At that point, she'd usually remind me that the one thing I always took to work with me was a blanket for all the sleeping I'd do on the job. Phyllis didn't think a big old wool blanket was an essential tool of the trade for a successful railroad career.

But then again, that's just her opinion.

- - - - - -

Early in our marriage when I was working on the Southern Pacific and we were living in California, there was never enough money. The electricity was constantly being shut off because we weren't paying our bill, and so was the water. That sure did piss Phyllis off. But not as much as the morning she looked out the window and saw me walking across the street in my underwear, our coffeepot in my hand, getting ready to fill that sucker up with our neighbor's hose.

And right here is an example of how two people can see the same exact event completely differently.

Phyllis thought I was embarrassing her and the family.

I thought I was being a good provider.

- - - - - -

$\mathcal{S}$eeing my brother single after his first marriage and seeing him now—how happy he is with his second wife, Deirdre, who's such a sweetheart—he's absolutely better off with Deirdre than he was as a bachelor. God, is he better off. In fact, seeing how happy he is, seeing the example he's setting the second time around, I know I could do better if I ever changed my mind and decided to get married again. This time around I know I could grade out much higher than a 4. On a scale of 1 to 10, I believe I could get as high as a 6.

And I'll tell you why: steady income.

You may think I'm making excuses here, but having your utilities constantly shut off puts an incredible strain on a marriage.

— — — — — —

I try to tell my sons all the time that the size of a woman's breasts shouldn't be all that important. I was saying that to my son Donny just the other day. But Donny said that if I'd been at the topless club with him the other night, watching guys stuff twenties into the panties of the girls with the biggest breasts, I might change my way of thinking. But you know what I was really thinking in that moment?

That's my boy.

— — — — — —

Sometimes you learn a valuable lesson in life after it's too late to help you. One of those lessons for me involved flowers. I'm telling you, it took ten years of a painful marriage for me to figure out that it doesn't hurt to send flowers to a woman once in a while. I do it with Phyllis now, even though we're divorced. For one thing I want her to be happy in her present marriage. And content.

But mostly I send them just so she never thinks about coming back.

—— —— —— —— —— ——

Part ✦ Four

The Great American Pastime

The closest thing I have to a drug of choice is football. I watch Thursday night college football on ESPN. I watch college football all day Saturday and into Saturday night. I watch pro football on the satellite all Sunday afternoon. I watch the Sunday night game and the Monday night game. A few weeks before the end of *Monday Night Football,* I can already start to feel myself getting depressed. Coming off the pro football season for me is like coming off heroin.

Which tells you a little bit about the full and exciting life I lead when I'm not at the shop.

There are only a few sports announcers I can tolerate without hitting the mute button. I like John Madden and I like listening to Al Michaels and Dan Dierdorf on *Monday Night Football*. I'm telling you, the rest of it is just the worst, most boring shit you've ever heard in your life. It's a whole afternoon of these morons telling you which guy fumbled the ball after you've just seen him fumble the goddamn ball. Hour after hour. Sports announcers should be like good company. They're supposed to be people you'd want to have over to watch the game.

Most of the guys they've got working now are so dumb, not just on the networks but on all these games I get with DSS channels, that if you ever saw them walking up to your house you'd be speed-dialing one of those militia groups.

— — — — — —

I'm all for women in sports. I always liked Billie Jean King and what she did for tennis and female athletes. Plus, as an entrepreneur myself, it's impossible not to spot some real good marketing and sales opportunities. Take the Women's National Basketball Association, for example. There are some cynics out there who think this might not sound evolved enough, but in my opinion the WNBA could do a lot better on television and at the box office if they could just add a few more supermodels who can dunk.

Short shorts wouldn't hurt the game any either. Swish.

- - - - - -

I've been making these sports picks—The Sports Lock of the Week—on Don's show for years. One day, when we were still in El Paso, a guy pulls up in the worst-looking kind of beat-up car you've ever seen in your life. It was like something out of *The Grapes of Wrath*. I thought he'd brought the car in hoping I could restore it. "You see that baby over there?" he said, pointing to the car. "I used to have a Mercedes until I started betting with you." I thought that showed a very bad attitude, not to mention a reckless disregard for the facts. My recollection is that my picks have been about 85 percent correct from the start.

Of course, if you believe that, you also probably think the Dalai Lama has a real job.

— — — — — —

People talk all the time about things that piss them off about sports. They don't like the money the athletes make, they don't like the owners, they don't like the agents. They don't like everyone's attitude. They don't like turning on the television and seeing another football star getting arrested with a bimbo or a bunch of dope on the coffee table. You know the only thing that pisses me off about sports?

When it's not on television.

Sometimes when I'm making a late-night whirlwind tour of all my television channels, I'll slow down and check out one of those shows where people wearing cowboy clothes line-dance. There is something hypnotic about watching couples, who seem fairly happy, rotate around a dance floor for four or five hours.

It seems wholesome. They don't appear drunk, and they are obviously not cheating on their spouses, or they wouldn't be on TV.

Although to be honest, I wouldn't mind seeing an occasional fight. It's like hockey . . . if they didn't punch the shit out of each other, it would be figure skating.

I

have to admit that I was a little late joining the national obsession with fitness. It's a real good idea, don't get me wrong. There aren't only tremendous benefits for your body, but your whole mental outlook. So I'm basically all for it, even if for most of my life my idea of aerobic exercise was walking out to my truck.

If I was looking for a real workout, I'd get into my truck and drive down to the convenience store for another pack of cigarettes and more sour-cream-and-onions dip.

- - - - - -

To be truthful, exercise shows on television wear my ass out.

I'll fall asleep on the couch after watching some sports event, wake up at three or four in the morning with one of those shows blaring in my face, and it will give me a scare on a par with the thought of getting married again.

I usually have to smoke half a pack of cigarettes just to calm myself down.

The only guy I really believe on the network news is Dan Rather. The thing about Rather that sets him apart is that people actually remember him being out in the field, whether he was in Vietnam or over there in Afghanistan with his face painted up like it was Halloween. I'd put him up against Tom Brokaw and Peter Jennings and the rest of them any day. Rather is the only legitimate new guy left. That's why I watch him.

When it's not football season, that is.

63

I don't like to repeat myself, but Rather really is the best newsman on television by far. Which for my money makes him the most trusted man in America, just as Walter Cronkite was on CBS before him. The fact that he's always ordering clothes and salsa from the Auto Body Express is just a coincidence.

And anybody who thinks otherwise is just another cynical sonofabitch.

$\mathbf{Y}$ou know the first thing that comes to mind when I think about the media? Piranhas. All of them swimming around, looking to make a killing with a story and not particularly interested in whether or not the story is true, whether it's about sex in the Oval Office or any other damn thing. From *Hard Copy* to *Inside Edition*, whether they're reporting on Clinton dropping his drawers or Mike Tyson's tendency to bite before he looks, all these piranhas think about is getting the story first. Get the story and worry later whether it's right. And I think most people who aren't in the media feel the exact same way.

Here's my formula for dealing with the piranhas on TV:

> 1. Assume 20 percent of what you see has some truth in it.

------

2. Assume the other 80 percent is bull-shit.

3. If less than 80 percent turns out to be true, you win.

4. Better yet, imagine the whole thing's a game show and you can't lose.

The O.J. stuff is exactly like football as far as I'm concerned. If I'm channel-surfing at night and see one of those lawyers, I always stop and watch. Alan Dershowitz was my favorite. You may not always agree with him, but he never changes his story the way the rest of them do. Most of them say something one week and three weeks later you'll see them on another show and they'll be saying something else. Dershowitz is a lot more believable than the others; at least he doesn't go around whining all the time like that tiresome Chris Darden, who came across to me as nothing but a whiny loser who should have found another line of work.

Darden goes around bitching so much I can't believe he never worked for me.

What I still don't get after Simpson got acquitted in that first trial is how anyone was allowed to sue him over the murders in the civil case. If they wanted to sue him it should have been over something completely different.

Being a terrible liar, for example.

Or for being the worst actor in the world.

Or maybe just for being an asshole.

- - - - - -

J ohnnie Cochran is as good at what he does as Don King is at promoting boxers. In fact, if the two of them switched jobs— King defending the killers, Cochran stealing from the fighters—would people really be able to tell the difference?

You know what baseball is good for?

Background noise.

No kidding, the game settles people down better than Prozac.

Or Al Gore.

I was listening to my brother's radio show one morning and heard Rock Newman, who manages the heavyweight boxer Riddick Bowe, saying that he thinks Jesus might have been black. I have no way of knowing whether that's true or not.

But if it is, basketball is a lot older game than we think.

I watch boxing all the time. My favorite boxer is Butterbean. He weighs 310 pounds, looks like the world's fattest bullet, fights in these four-round bouts, and just kills people. Larry Merchant, the slightly annoying, often confused boxing commentator, called him a fat phony. I think Butterbean is great. He was making two hundred bucks a week until he started fighting in these Toughman contests. Now he's knocking down a couple hundred grand a fight.

Is this a great country, or what?

Larry might have been wrong about Butterbean, but he was right about this: a mariachi band was playing in the ring before a fight between two 106-pound Mexicans about to beat the shit out of each other. About halfway through a song that was threatening to go on as long as "Stairway to Heaven," Larry says, "This sucks."

The network made him apologize because their fucking PC Police thought he was offending

- - - - - -

Mexicans. Had it been Yanni or John Tesh, he could have said the same thing and they would have all agreed and he would have also been right.

It did suck.

I't's always painful for me to get to the spring and realize that there's still five months to go until football season. So every year I start telling myself that this will be the year when I become a baseball fan again, which I haven't been since Sandy Koufax, the last pitcher worth a shit, was with the Dodgers. I even ordered up this package of games I saw advertised on the satellite where you get something like a season's ticket at the ballpark, a thousand games or so, for only a hundred dollars.

Knowing me, I won't watch any of the games, but it was too damn good a deal to pass up.

Right now at the Auto Body Express I have just about the best set of employees you could ever have. Believe me, it didn't happen overnight. It took about four years to put the current crew together. Kind of makes me more sympathetic to some of those poor bastards trying to put a sports team together.

If it was this hard for me, I can only imagine what a nightmare it is when you have to keep a bunch of young millionaire assholes happy, not to mention winning a few games in the process.

Part ✦ Five

Politics

Last time around I voted for Bob Dole because I liked him and respected him, even though I knew he didn't have any real answers for the country either.

None of them do.

The day I voted for Dole, this was my thinking: I'm about to vote for a guy who still thinks it's 1957.

What's not to like?

— — — — — —

Everyone acted like it was supposed to be some big dilemma the night the verdict came down in O.J.'s civil trial whether to watch the verdict or President Clinton's State of the Union address back in '97. My feeling all night was: what dilemma, exactly? I watched every minute of the O.J. deal and so did the rest of the country. People at the shop told me the next day that I wasn't being a good citizen. I told them I'd already been a good citizen.

Like I said, I voted for Dole.

- - - - - - -

I'm sorry, but from the outset nobody outside of Washington, D.C., cared about Whitewater. I frankly don't understand why the media spent so much time on that. For my money, I say let's bring back Gennifer Flowers, find out what really went on with her and Clinton back in Arkansas. After all, that's when Clinton began pursuing his real dream in earnest.

Like breaking all of Wilt Chamberlain's records—for getting laid.

The whole country's gone cynical. I can't tell sometimes whether people have just given up thinking things can get better, or whether they just don't give a shit. It's probably too close to call. But the more you talk to people, you get the feeling that they have given up . . . except the ones answering those polls, telling some asshole in a gray suit how fucking happy they are. Folks have given up on schools, on politicians, on religion, and on each other. It seems like we're bombarded with another scandal every day. And it gets to feel like there's nothing you can count on in this world.

Except maybe my brother's radio show, of course. And me, his best guest. Did I mention that?

I promise you I'm not being cynical here, but anybody who tells you that O.J. being a football star didn't affect the way they looked at the whole thing is lying. It sure as hell affected the way I looked at the whole thing. I'd followed this guy since he was a star in junior college. Then in college at USC, then during his whole career in the pros. I can remember, when I was younger, I used to lay off work (and Phyllis can attest to that) just to watch O.J. run with the ball in those USC–Notre Dame games. You absolutely cannot divorce yourself from the feelings that you used to have, I don't care how hard you try.

There wasn't a single day I watched either trial when I didn't find myself thinking, "Goddamnit, Juice, what happened to you?"

You know what did amuse the hell out of me the night of the civil verdict? Watching all the cops outside the courthouse. Police helicopters flying overhead. Motorcycle cops everywhere you looked. All of them supposedly there for security, which ostensibly meant protecting O.J. You know what I kept thinking?

How many of those cops would actually have unholstered their guns if Fred Goldman or someone tried to pull a Dirty Harry?

Here's my plan for O.J.

to make about fifty million dollars, pay off all his debts, and finance a whole new life in some country other than this one: one more book.

Title?

I Did It.

Here's what the book would be about:

1. How the bastard did it.
2. Why he thought he could get away with it.
3. How to kill two people in a few minutes, keep them quiet while you do, and still have time to get ready for your flight to Chicago.

I'd pay twenty-five bucks, or whatever a hardcover book costs these days, just to find out what the real timeline was. Hell, I'd buy that before I'd read another piece-of-shit book by one of those lawyers.

Sometimes, watching the trial, I kept expecting Oliver Stone or someone to step into the courtroom and yell, "Cut." Then O.J. would take a big bow, Ron and Nicole would walk in, you know like that Orson Welles's deal with *War of the Worlds.* The way the media treated the trial it started to seem like someone's idea of entertainment. The whole damn thing felt like something they made up.

Except, at the end of the day, those two people are still dead.

The very last thing I thought before I turned off the television the night of the guilty verdict was this: Where does Geraldo go from here?

Of course, that was before Clinton ended up with his pants around his ankles, and you had to hose Geraldo down all over again.

H

ere's a way to understand the entire Whitewater investigation, as far as I can figure out: Which goober knew about what loan, and when? And who screwed who out of what?

You know, like every other business deal in America.

— — — — — —

I actually like Hillary Clinton. I know a lot of people don't, but the more I know about her, the more I do. She's a good mother, that's one thing. It's obvious she's done a good job raising that kid. And she's got that stand-by-your-man thing going for her, because she's stuck by that creep she's married to.

If she doesn't mind that her husband is trying to break all of Wilt's screwing records, why should I?

- - - - - -

You know something else I like about the First Lady? (That's if she's still the First Lady by the time this book comes out and not in some minimum-security prison.) As much as she gets attacked, and she gets it right between the eyes on a fairly regular basis, she hangs in there and never complains. She takes whatever punches the media throw her way like a man.

One night during a boxing match when that heavyweight boxer Oliver McCall broke down in the ring and started crying, I actually remember thinking, "Jesus, man, get a grip. We've got a First Lady who's got more balls than you."

And I'll tell you one other thing: In a fair fight, she would kick Kenneth Starr's ass.

— — — — — —

I wasn't aware until all the news about Clinton and his fund-raising tactics came out—before all the stuff about him and Monica Lewinsky came out—that they basically operate the White House the way you do a Holiday Inn. As it turns out, 1600 Pennsylvania Avenue has just about everything you need except a front desk, a concierge, and a bellhop.

If you ask me, the way they move high rollers in and out of the Lincoln Bedroom, they should set some kind of frequent-traveler points like they give you at the Marriott, or offer up a VIP card like I have for the Super 8 Motel.

— — — — — —

I think the Clintons' work it this way at the White House: They don't openly solicit money, but you're supposed to know the deal. Like if you call downstairs and order room-service coffee for two, that's $25,000. Lunch goes for $50,000. If you want to watch a movie in your room, that's $100,000.

And if you want to *make* a movie in your room . . . well, there are those frisky interns.

= = = = = =

Mo kidding, the next thing you know, they'll be running bimbos in and out of the guest rooms at the White House, the way they do if you're a high roller in Vegas.

Well, more bimbos.

Sometimes I think there must be a big smoky room somewhere in the White House that looks like one of the lounges at Caesars Palace.

The more you find out about Clinton, the better Richard Nixon looks in comparison.

Nixon just lied *sometimes*.

It's getting to where Clinton lies every time he opens his mouth, at least in a nonBig Mac situation.

- - - - - -

The thing that actually worries me the most about everything in the White House being up for sale is that Clinton might get it into his head to go into the mail-order business. You know, using some Arkansas pig for a logo, selling pork rinds and Cheez Whiz.

Good thing his brother's a total loser or I might actually worry.

Bill Clinton was as obsessed with getting reelected in 1996 as Richard Nixon was in 1972. He just didn't have a bunch of thugs break into the Democratic National Committee offices at the Watergate.

He had Al Gore dialing for dollars instead, plus so many Chinese guys running around the White House it looked like they were trying to break some sort of record for take-out.

Little did we know at the time, of course, that the Chinese would be just, well, the appetizers. Scandal-wise, I mean. There was a time before all the Monica business, and after all the Gennifer business, when you wondered if Clinton could ever find the time to get laid.

I, for one, am glad he's back to being my kind of President, which means he's got his priorities in place (blow jobs being high on the list—very high).

- - - - - -

Janet Reno being Attorney General of the United States is so scary and unbelievable, I don't even know what to think about it sometimes. That woman rising to the top of her field is one of the most amazing things that's ever happened in government in my lifetime. Forget about the Peter Principle. That's over. It's the Reno Principle from here on.

Put it another way, I wouldn't let Janet Reno put the tops on my damn salsa jars.

— — — — — —

You know who I do kind of like in Clinton's administration, or at least from the alumni association? That little squirrel Dick Morris. I know he took a lot of heat and ended up losing his job when they caught him in the hotel with a hooker, wearing a dog collar and leash. Everybody sort of rushed to judgment on the poor bastard, the way we always do when some sex scandal breaks. I think we should have stepped back and maybe not reacted so hastily.

Of course, that may just be on account of my fondness for collars, leashes, and dogs in general.

- - - - - - -

I've reached the point with Clinton where I don't even want to be bothered by any accusations until somebody can come up with an impeachable offense. Or the big one, as I like to think about it. For instance, I never thought Paula Corbin Jones had a case, though I do think she performed a real public service with the President, even if it wasn't the public service he was looking for in that hotel room.

I mean, who knew before this happened that it was wrong to drop your drawers in front of the help?

— — — — — — —

I know a lot of people think that Al Gore is going to succeed Clinton in the White House someday, but as far as I'm concerned that doofus is never going to be President. The thing that finally clinched it for me was finding out about all the telemarketing he did to raise money in 1996. On the other hand, given how good he is working the phones, he might consider a second career down here at the Auto Body Express.

He wouldn't be the first person to get a new lease on life selling T-shirts and salsa.

The guy I'd actually like to see run for the Democrats in 2000 is Bill Bradley. I know it's unheard of to have a politician without any baggage, but I think we could all get used to it with Bradley. It might be refreshing to have a guy who's on the up-and-up, who isn't a tool, who knows his stuff, and, by the way, was one of the best forwards to ever shoot hoops.

On the other hand, horny hillbilly white trash like Bill Clinton is a tough act to follow.

Somebody asked me not long ago what I thought Bob Dole was doing these days. I don't know why, but I have a picture in my mind of him in the backyard standing next to a barbecue, flipping tiny weenies, and sucking down some kind of nonalcoholic brew.

I know this might sound selfish to you and somewhat self-absorbed, but if he is, I hope he's still wearing his Auto Body Express blue denim work shirt.

Part · Six

Women

I figure I can joke about women all I want because I don't have a chauvinistic bone in my body (well, maybe one). I treat men and women exactly the same. Especially the ones who work for me. I don't know why we need to pass Equal Rights Amendments in this country. Anybody with any common sense at all can see how well things work when you don't discriminate against anybody. Hell, it's easy. I don't believe in discrimination in the workplace because I don't believe in discrimination anywhere. O.K., so maybe it's true that I've occasionally offered estrogen to a couple of the women who work for me, but that's just me trying to help. Actually, I tell all the women at the Auto Body Express to think of the Petty Cash Box as the Estrogen Box. The money's there if they need it.

People who say I don't have a nurturing side don't know shit about me.

— — — — — —

H

aving lived into my fifties somehow, I have had a lot of time to think about the differences between men and women, outside of the obvious one. The biggest difference that I can see is that women deal with life on an emotional level, while men are much more practical about things. Men, for example, will look at $2 + 2$ and almost always come up with 4.

With women, it's my experience that $2 + 2$ can equal almost any goddamn thing.

- - - - - -

People may think this is a little bit sexist, but I'm just offering an opinion here: Marcia Clark could make a lot more money walking down Hollywood Boulevard at midnight than she's ever going to make as a lawyer. If it's true that she and Chris Darden had a romance during the O.J. trial, it must have been like my marriage to Phyllis.

Bitch, bitch, bitch.

Speaking of hard to figure women, I'm still trying to understand how Denise Brown, Nicole Brown Simpson's sister, could keep going on *Larry King* and *Geraldo* and slobber all over the place, then pull herself together in time to go celebrate at Elaine's.

She's either working on some grief therapy I'm not familiar with, or maybe just getting away from Larry and Geraldo makes her want to party more than Madonna.

Here's another tip

about women, one that I've learned the hard way: If you can possibly avoid it, don't live with one. It doesn't mean that I don't like women. I do. Don't get me wrong. It's just that by the fourth or fifth day of any kind of extended togetherness I tend to get a bit antsy for the visit to end. She can usually tell. Maybe it's when I start saying things like "Hey, do we need to do any laundry before we start to pack your suitcase?" Or when I ask her on Tuesday what time her Friday flight leaves again.

Basically, my relationship with Four-Legged Fred is about as complicated a relationship as I can handle. With Fred, I'll guarantee you one damn thing: He never says, "I don't feel we're connecting the way we used to," then running out of the room crying.

God, I love this dog.

N o man I know goes more than ten minutes without thinking about sex, whether they want to admit it or not. Women, on other hand, don't really start enjoying sex until they mature and get into their forties. Not only do they start to like it, they actually start thinking about it too.

Which, if you think about it, makes them a lot more like men at that point.

- - - - - - -

O ne time my brother had these two women on the show who'd written this best-seller about rules for dating. That got me to thinking about my own rules and some romantic tips that have always worked for me:

Rule Number One: Act like you don't give a shit. (In other words never, ever, offer to wash your girlfriend's car.)

Rule Number Two: The more independent they are, the better off you are. (Think of it this way: her cash flow or yours.)

Rule Number Three: Keep yourself clean. (Never underestimate the power of a bar of Ivory soap.)

I was having the following conversation the other night with a woman I've been seeing for years.

She says, "Did you take your vitamins?"

I say, "I'll take them when I'm ready."

She says, "If you don't take your vitamins, I'm going home." (A flight of about two thousand miles.)

You know what all this means? While I wasn't looking a real good woman had turned into a wife. And if I ever write another country song, that's the title.

I don't want to dwell on this whole deal about keeping yourself as clean as possible as a way to successful romance, but I still might be married to Phyllis if I'd just kept myself up a little better. It just happened to take me a little longer than other people to know what a big deal changing your shirt can be. Or taking a shower once a day. You know what the message is here: Stay on top of the little things. In other words, you don't always have to have an expensive piece of jewelry in your hand.

Just a simple bar of Ivory.

(There are exceptions to this rule, of course. There's this woman Laura Ingraham from CBS News that my brother has on his radio show all the time. She's made a pretty big name for herself because of her Republican politics. I wouldn't be surprised if her idea of foreplay is getting a Rolex off a guy's wrist.)

I was married to Phyllis for ten years, and I've been seeing the same woman for about the last five, but there have been long stretches of my life when I was unattached. Those periods gave me a chance to try out some of my favorite pickup lines on women. Here's one: "Hey, I've got three or four hundred dollars in my pocket." That one has never let me down. Another line I'd use when I didn't want to get involved in a particularly lengthy conversation: "Hey, why don't you just tell me right now about how much this is going to cost." But you know I'm feeling especially romantic and ready to sweep a woman off her feet when I use this one: "Why don't we come back to my place and listen to one of my country albums and then have sex."

I guess that's the old Cary Grant coming out in me.

- - - - - - -

I don't want to make it sound as if I'm against safe sex here, but I've never owned a condom. Here's why: If I'm not sure about the person, I'm out of there. That's the deal. If I'm even vaguely worried that having sex with a woman might kill me, I'm on my way home.

I guess my definition of safe sex is parking myself on the couch and watching TV with the dogs.

My idea of a romantic weekend away would go something like this: I'd find an out-of-the-way cabin in some remote spot that the rest of the world hasn't discovered yet and the tourist scum hasn't ruined. Ideally, it would be someplace so remote that you'd have to drive to it for several hours, even after you've gotten off the plane. I'd bring along good eats, salsa and chips, you name it. Then here's what I do.

Go there alone.

- - - - - - -

Part ✦ Seven

Fred's Best
Friend

Since everybody knows how devoted I am to Four-Legged Fred, I've often been asked this question: If I was forced to choose between Four-Legged Fred and a beautiful woman, who would I pick?

The dog wins hands down.

Let me put it another way: If a good-looking woman were drowning and so was Four-Legged Fred, I would swim out and save Four-Legged Fred every single time, and I'll tell you why.

The dog has never thrown a single kitchen utensil at me.

I don't want to sound as if I'm not evolved when it comes to women. All I'm saying is that dogs are much more low-maintenance. For example, they're not going to go on for two days about my forgetting to put the goddamn milk away. With a dog, you know that if you pet him a couple of times, the bastard goes off and lies down happy. Out of everybody I've ever lived with, Four-Legged Fred is far and away the easiest.

I'm not saying we don't have our power struggles in bed, but who doesn't?

- - - - - -

I have three other dogs beside Four-Legged Fred.

There's also Larry, Phyllis, and Pasok, my killer guard dog.

Not one of them is invited to the afterlife with me.

In fact, after what Larry did the other day after I forgot to let him out, he can go straight to hell.

- - - - - -

When I first got Pasok, he was more than a little hyper. After all, he had never been near people and was trained as an attack dog. I've had to work with him a lot, acclimating him to the Auto Body Express and the cast of characters who keep coming through with their, what shall we say, big mouths. Pasok kept biting people at first (fortunately, my insurance covers dog bites), especially if they talked real loud or moved too quickly. When I explained all this to the vet, he suggested that the dog was trying to establish dominance. But it looks like I've got things under control now.

I guess you could call me the alpha Fred of this here little pack.

A while back, my attack dog Pasok developed a problem with his coat. His solution was to lick himself, nearly nonstop. I think you and a White House intern know where. Anyway, the vet came by to check him out. While the vet was examining the dog, he asked a number of questions, including had we put Pasok out to stud.

I explained that if anybody was gonna get laid, it wasn't gonna be the fucking dog. The vet seemed annoyed, and pointed out that it was the dog who was licking himself.

Sure, I said, because he can.

- - - - - -

Four-Legged Fred isn't always a saint, by the way. He has his moods too. He'll get up in the morning pissed off about something and stay pissed off all day while I have to guess why.

Now that I think about it, Four-Legged Fred is a lot more like my wife Phyllis than I care to admit.

I bought a new wallet the other day and put it down on the dresser. When I came back later, that goddamn Larry had chewed up not only the wallet but also my VIP card for the Super 8 Motel. Now, I usually cut Larry more slack than I do the other dogs, because he actually seems to care about me. But then the first time I turn my head, he's into my wallet and chewing up my credit cards.

I'll say it again: I might as well be married to him.

— — — — — —

Part · Eight

100% Fred

*C*oming from the Southwest, I'm very sympathetic to the plight of Native Americans, and have been my whole life. I know what the government has done to them. I know every single way they've been screwed. But I have to be honest about something: These guys can piss you off as easily as anyone else can.

In fact, it's getting to where you can't tell Native Americans from any other kind of Americans.

— — — — — —

The only place you will find more New Age nuts than you do at a John Tesh concert is Santa Fe, New Mexico. People used to tell me it was one of the coolest and most fashionable places on earth. Then I moved here, and discovered the only difference between Santa Fe and El Paso is about three thousand feet.

And that a lot of the folks here sit on the wrong end of the bar stool.

I keep hoping that when the rappers start shooting at each other next time, John Tesh's piano will get caught just once in the cross fire. Don't get me wrong: I don't wish any harm on Tesh himself. Just that piano of his. It doesn't even have to be a rapper. It could be one of those suicide bombers.

You want to make the world a better place, start there.

- - - - - - -

They've done a good job with country music, making it appeal to a wider audience. But what they've done is create something where just about everybody sounds like everybody else. You can watch TNN at night and not have any idea who's doing the singing. In the old days, whether it was Don Williams or George Jones or Ray Price or Merle Haggard, all you had to do was hear the first note of a song and you'd know who it was immediately. Now they all sound alike. And what they really sound like is a bunch of guys who could have fit right in singing pop music in the sixties. When I was growing up, you had the idea that country singers were real cowboys.

Now you can see them sitting around with the cast of *Friends* ordering up another one of those decaffeinated cappuccinos. (Hi, I'm Garth Brooks, I'd like a decaf mocha lattè, please?)

Shit.

I can't understand why people make such a big deal out of Ellen DeGeneres coming out as a lesbian and then turning her sitcom character into a lesbian as well. The way things are going in life and the way the world has changed, all of this seems perfectly natural to me.

But that just may be the Santa Fe coming out in me.

When I heard there'd
been a mass suicide at Rancho Santa Fe a couple
of years ago, I got real excited. But that's only because I didn't hear the "Rancho" part.

Alot of people I know are scared to death of UFOs, especially in the Southwest.

I never have been.

It's the people who *believe* in UFOs who scare the shit out of me.

On the other hand, I will read *anything* about the Mob. I mean anything. I will read any book, watch any movie, check out any Mob documentary—A&E, The Food Network, whatever . . . they cover it, I cover them.

They should let John Gotti out of jail just long enough for him to whack Sammy "The Bull" Gravano. Right there's a book, a movie, and two TV shows, not to mention getting rid of a fucking stool-pigeon asshole.

I'm so jacked up about the Mob, I drive around with a blowup doll in the trunk of my car. Okay, so maybe that's not the only reason she's back there. Whatever.

— — — — — —

One more thing: I have only attended one awards show in my entire life, when "I Don't Want to Have to Marry You" won the Music City Song of the Year Award. It was one of the great nights of my life. I got to meet Ernest Tubb, Barbara Mandrell, Crystal Gayle, Johnny Paycheck, people like that whom I've always admired. The only bad part of the night was when I had to go up in front of all those people and accept my award. Somehow I pulled myself together and gave the only kind of speech that anybody ever wants to hear at an awards show, from the Oscars on down. I said "Thank you" and sat my ass down.

And if I win any book awards for this little gem, I promise to do the same thing.

Epilogue

‑‑‑‑‑‑‑‑‑

At the end of a book like this, I guess you're supposed to sum things up. But I'm not going to wear you out with a bunch of self-serving bull shit, other than to tell you this: You don't have to change. People are always trying to make other people improve themselves, give up smoking, do aerobics, quit drinking, etc. But look at me. I stuck to my program of doing as little as possible besides watching sports and hanging out with the dogs and things have turned out pretty well for me.

Of course, if somebody did put me in charge of the world for one day and told me I could pass any law I wanted to, this would be it: Pay teachers and cops like ballplayers. Make them the millionaires instead of the Dennis Rodmans and Al-

‑ ‑ ‑ ‑ ‑ ‑

bert Belles. And the cops who work in the inner city, I'd pay them like Michael Jordan. Otherwise I wouldn't find myself messing with much.

If you couldn't tell by now, I'm a live-and-let-live kind of guy. Just going out to sit with my horses—Phyllis and Fred—in the early evening, not doing anything except maybe smoking an occasional cigarette while we watch the sun set, suits me just fine. And listening in to my brother's radio program, especially when he's talking about the Auto Body Express. And there's one more thing that makes my heart skip a beat—hearing the phones ring off the hook.

That number, again, is 1-800-272-1957.

God bless you, and drive safely.

The End

FRED IMUS, Two-Legged Fred, is a staple on his brother Don's *Imus in the Morning* talk-radio show, syndicated in over one hundred markets around the nation and simulcast on MSNBC. Fred lives in Santa Fe, where he runs his highly lucrative catalog company, the Auto Body Express. But before that, he mostly restored '57 Chevys when he had the cash, ragged on his ex-wife, and not much else.

MIKE LUPICA writes four syndicated columns a week for the *New York Daily News*. He is also a contributing writer for *ESPN Magazine* and a regular on *Good Morning America* and ESPN's Sunday morning *Sports Reporters* show. He is the author of a number of books, the latest being *Mad as Hell*.